WITHDRAWN

AS BURNING LEAVES

AS BURNING LEAVES

GABRIEL JESIOLOWSKI

poems

 Red Hen Press | *Pasadena, CA*

Book design by Cassidy Trier

Library of Congress Cataloging-in-Publication Data

Names: Jesiolowski, Gabriel, author.
Title: As burning leaves / Gabriel Jesiolowski.
Description: First edition. | Pasadena, CA : Red Hen Press, 2017. | "Poetry."
  | Includes bibliographical references.
Identifiers: LCCN 2016048407 | ISBN 9781597090254 (pbk. : alk. paper)
Classification: LCC PS3610.E85 A6 2017 | DDC 811/.6—dc23
LC record available at https://lccn.loc.gov/2016048407

The National Endowment for the Arts, the Los Angeles County Arts Commission, the Dwight Stuart Youth Fund, the Max Factor Family Foundation, the Pasadena Tournament of Roses Foundation, the Pasadena Arts & Culture Commission and the City of Pasadena Cultural Affairs Division, the City of Los Angeles Department of Cultural Affairs, the Audrey & Sydney Irmas Charitable Foundation, Sony Pictures Entertainment, Amazon Literary Partnership, and the Sherwood Foundation partially support Red Hen Press.

First Edition
Published by Red Hen Press
www.redhen.org

for the fighters + healers

CONTENTS

III

AS BURNING LEAVES

I

In the palm
the seed
is burned up
in the wind.

—Amiri Baraka

ENTRY FOR THE MEDIAN STRIP

it may help us to remember that our breath is not synchronized, not elegant, as we fuck on the edge of the median strip between highway & farmland—even on the plane field of the sheets my knees are buckling, but the gutters are manmade—my eyes lost in the stucco cast of the roofline—the rushing of the rain in the gutters, *manmade*—I want her to register on my skin—every house on the street, *manmade*, every war & war plane, *manmade*, the fluid gestures of her hands in saltwater, even the wind in the tunnel is *manmade*

∧

the wind here, the carved vessel of the canoe here
thousands of days, thousands of gutted fish, every time
the birds dove to the highway

I want to return, I ask my mother, to the rooftop,
that I let a man enter, speak for me, it was something he said—
something out of his mouth that I would take

∧

VISIBLE WORLD

∧

we row out to the center of the lake to be among the fir spires
blue—the loon's voice
                              wind moves the leaves across the water
            they do not gather / do not cling

        the solitude surrounds   us long & deft

∧

years later, I exhale into a tree what lore is left
        of you

dissolve thirty-four of your letters in transparent bags filled with creek water
            the words that used to seduce me, that now wound me
            lift in ribbons of ink, serene & adrift

was there a line
        black bark, blossoms in the mild rain, smelling like piss

∧

        I ease up on your pressed
        collar as
                I no longer straighten it to offer you to the visible world

FIELDED

nine
scarring rituals

the female oak tree
slit into with verse

so faint is the here / the after
outside—the trees are drained for sap

TEMPORARY LANDMARK

∧

do not look at the mud-hard scarves around my shoulders   or the outcast
sky that follows

you should lose your bearings altogether
your broken touch : a temporary landmark

my body weary of all of the thunder rumbling through the chest the way
her wineglass is weary of holding wine

∧

what is the difference between a calendar
          & our breathing

∧

continues to scar
this white wing
in the center of my eyes

∧

words wing span
between us
smoke
between us
high water
between us

you would say *come hell*
or high water

I wait like a child in this town

without the compass I move into another body
that does not erase my own, for all this time
I have tried to dissolve the

periphery

the walls with leaves made of shadow
your bed muted by the barren pine
two Buddhas back to

back

I grid the coordinates of our
separation as though stars
as burning

leaves

lately I make no effort to salvage statues or vessels
all of the letters that I write to you
return nothing to its place

RED CLAY

because I am done comparing

because our lungs need the rest

because ice will form over bramble

because the drawings are footnotes

because I write with a rag across my chest

because I will return to gather, disperse & let go of my things

because according to the *book of changes*, tonight you pattern yourself

     after the grey sea & I dive beneath the boat trying to pull up

     the radical weight of the anchor

because I imagine you rising from someone else's bed

because a stranger leans into me, because his arms are near somber,

     the twilight courting us

because I have taken four shots of whiskey into my throat & this margin

because I don't precaution that rain will flood the field, the rain floods

     the field / because the air is bitter as an apple core / because

     you've never seen my hands stained with red clay

because of my nerves / because he made a wreath of bittersweet &

     vines while he was driving here /

because the embers are most beautiful when

     breathing out

because of strangers

because of the shape of coins

VAGABOND

covered in frost
this window / days of over
sleeping staring into a concrete
hereafter /
rented *Vagabond* again   in the first scene she is frozen
in a ditch   her body is measured, her hair pulled away from her
face /   I wait for the scene when she is trying to live with a
sheepherder   he asks if she wants to grow potatoes   he
gives her a plot of land
of course she never uses it / instead she sleeps into late morning hours
in a trailer beside his worn stone house—
without law, without

LESS

if you take up drawing   [route as drawing, drawing as route]
if the vine of charcoal does not break as you drag it across your stomach
if you round the edge of the calm-faced lake   [if you never send the letters, which
                                                              are porous]

                    less
if you are held beneath
                                                                    less somehow
if you carry the loaves of bread as though they are timber

                    less
if you dare winter
if you cut a star into your leg
if you find the green in the muck

less if the clouds disperse to allow   blue inlets

IN THE CABIN IN MAINE

we fuck standing
in the shower
stall paneled
dark with mold
holes from
mites beam
light through
the raw
pine

how
little
I know
in the dim
shower stall
where the fish
are sometimes
cut

MONARCH SEASON

^

envelope with stitching

arrives in late September

how was I ever impenetrable

now—   I'm like a cloud

^

distant foghorns   rotting lettuce
the erotic stain of ivy on a brick wall

between us   :   ages of grey waves

^

your law of silence /
the red trees start up at once—a chorus   monarchs have died together these last four
days   I find them floating
downward in the field

^

to travel the roads
alone
to buy a beige jacket

I am learning a second language

. . . all the salt in the air

you have left

    dew in barrels

    the causeways between

    fucking & nothingness

        Virginia Woolf's

    weeping-hair

    bookmarking

        the page on

            the thickening

            ash world

you have left

    my climbing barefoot over your hip

        bones / the hiss & spit of the radiator / your teeth

        on my clit

            the weight of clamshells

you have left

        the wading in / the pouring through

    & chance, critical chance

            plain-faced you have left

ENTRY FOR A WREN

in the photograph she stands at the edge of a pier: wields the sky as a wren—this image cannot withstand her—for my body, haunting comes in waves, dark ones, has little or no memory—I lie on the table with the needles pulling slightly from my skin—she touches the oak doors & around the troubled windows—she palms the shingles, licks the dew on the house (each small eye)—she collapses the space where the ravine lifts from the bell of the earth . . . in the photograph the light is falling or has failed—it may have failed in the negative or only from the eye's quivering

A HIGHWAY BACK

broken-line road where I'd rest my head on your thighs   you would wake
me to see a formation of birds descending to the rusted rail of the highway
route   so close to
dreaming   these
days, the bruises flowering   not hesitant to

                        exist

II

branches exist, wind lifting them exists,
and the lone drawing made by the branches

of the tree called an oak tree exists,
of the tree called an ash tree, a birch tree,
a cedar tree, the drawing repeated

in the gravel garden path; weeping
exists as well

—Inger Christensen, translated by Susanna Nied

STONES DO NOT MATTER

For Dario Núñez Ameni & a more fluid architecture.

I.

the folk song says that we need a little sadness—   so we invent the passing of

         railcars   the oxidation reduction of raku, the taste

of beets & sugar

        we invent the loss of your blue eyes flaming at the corneas

II.

it's the geography of the body that leaves us talking:

            I bind my breasts today & stare

               at the ground

so what of the architects who mourn their buildings   so what of the market

square   my feet arching in & out

        I keep assuring the air / that cuts into the wings of birds

CLIMATES

in the Turkish film he walks away from her   months later
       he waits for her in drifting snow banks / their hair
is the same length / neither smile when they see each other
       the fragility of each sound . . .   the hotel room has dark
burnt red floors   a missing drawer—nothing can go back
exactly—each of them, in their very separate grief
quietly smoking, drinking coffee   from marble
                       vases

FAR

the air is brittle with
bird song

my earth, your earth, is parallel
though

we cannot hear the scratches
in records

or the sound of the copper library door
closing

I read aloud the four grievances
which leads

devotion
far astray

in the end, which I know has a lot to do with the way that wind moves the leaves & all
of the carrying we have been doing—there is low ground & no one speaking

but first, we'll have to wade through the root systems of abandoned houses, cold drives,
drinking alone—we will lie with lovers who are sudden strangers, the moon that loses tide

& supposing you are lucky . . . there is the salt air too, maybe a spool of five hundred
starlings that move in & out of the light, if lucky, someone may brush your arm & say

under their breath—*I wish I could go home*: but empathy usually ends as abruptly as it
began because no one can breathe into your mouth for that long without

losing their own sense of balance & with so many casualties, it's important to wring
out your hands under the steam of the kettle & in fact, in a photograph, a woman

had tied all of her neighbor's tea kettles to her body: this would be a place to begin
rethinking a life—to let the steam engender the body . . . all of your illusions, your grace

& sense of not belonging coiled into the days that pass with an innocence so acute
that there seems a fine line between being recognized somehow & entirely unknown

RETURN TO FORM

stray & strange,
I climbed the narrow
stairs of his rowhouse—
smoke hesitated from
a single candle

he held my shoulders down
between the church &
billboard in Lawrenceville
the houses rose in light up
the surrounding slopes

his clothes had a maudlin
heaviness (he was wearing
too much tweed) which
reminded me that he
had lived alone for a while

descending the staircase
car in the alley again without wings
sky without perfect architecture
the stubborn, unweildy boy inside of me
my nipples sore & hard against my blouse
planes casting shadows

LOVE IS WHAT YOU MADE IT OUT TO BE

slow night of salt—that desire / recreates: stags cross the border

—Coral Bracho

you speak gingerly in last night's dream:

come lie on this raft . . .
these fish bones will support you

then, I whispered that I would *take*

my hands off for you

upon waking

the black sky was dark blue

I was followed

then I couldn't remember how to kiss

^

ash through my fingertips
does rain fall in empty doorways
do you wash your clothing
with the weight of your body
pine needles gather on
solitary ground
I keep
losing the birds
who climb into the heavy
ardor of the trees

^

woke up
trembling, the hall

way   of sawdust-air

streets blown

backward   in memorial

from a phone
booth I learn that
you did not

know

that I was inside of a mountain
we were apart
there was

nothing

to be done

ENTRY FOR ILLUSORY SPACE

I try not to open my eyes through Ohio—I wear my mother's scarf with the tooth-
like stitching—the ice formed around the branches guides us deep into loneliness—
fruits all dark—I've started the injections—I wait for my upper lip to quiver less, to
roll my shoulders back & feel their peaks touch—I try to act as if there was no where
to go, no one to be—I have injured all my saints—the terracotta mouth, imaginary
space charged with the dogged curve of memory—when a dark wave is coming—I
can feel my breath in the hallways beneath the earth—she says never to injure the
collarbone—as it holds you up :

the antler of the body

FRENETIC SPINE

pages with teeth marks, cocaine, blue-grey pills, idling smoke
around a tin can punctured in the shape of a bowhead whale—

how in momentary disbelief I have taken up with someone else
we don't bathe or care what is broken

I still call out to you from the scarred rocks of the East River
send you sandalwood soap, ink drawings on pillowcases, the frenetic spine of a fish

below my window, when I wake, the moonlit streets are covered
in clothing & I wonder: what if there is no ghost realm?

what if the wind has always been alone with the wind?

ENTRY FOR FASTING

take the clothing out of teak drawers—wear mostly cotton the color of brown bags—
take me out of here—all day I have been writing script over a mattress my sister gave
to me—the green tea tastes as bitter as a cut—I used to have dreams in which I was
covered in flour . . . are these dreams useful?—when I was young, writing a poem
after rape, I took from Olga Broumas when she says in "foreigner" *up small woman
alone / icicles / naked*—I want to separate the land from my body—though I sleep &
am lost in sleep

I HAVEN'T

I.

been watching the shoreline—landlocked, again—the pine shower stall was a set—
a soulless wood crate that momentarily held the water back

was my mouth full of words the way a barn is full of hay grass—I didn't speak for a
while—& when we made love you were a dagger—I menstruated quietly, trying not
to composite myself—in your absence that summer there was a long plank—I drove
a lot through cricketed meta roads—believe me that we were not in each other—not
like the fen of blue over white engravings—not like the sky in our bodies or the burnt
fry pan, black & rose

II.

somehow, the body ceases grieving—geese pattern to the mountain crags—
the distance between your cunt & throat: the length of a bolt of silk

NAMES FOR TOUCH WE NEVER USED

I want to let go into the cold, Camus   *live to the point of tears*
                    so I preserve the loneliest parts of the body

                    the dog's blue, inner-ear tattoo
                    your ribs, a finger apart

in the brick house, some evenings we would pass our names into each other's mouths

                              ∧

            even if no one will speak to me   I want not to be spoken to

ENTRY FOR ORDINARY SADNESS

suppose you sway this way & that way—the tide is out so you walk slow along the momentary edge—each clamshell ignored—been a while since desire has hooked you—a while since grief (in the thinness of morning fog) retched you—though the landscape wears a veil—you know there is something beyond market value but are late to capitalism—ashamed by the smell of money & the empty weight of your breasts

VINES / BIRTH

there are only three Yangtze turtles left
& I was born today, only with a stronger jaw

you write to me of ice as I walk from
florist to florist asking to arrange vines

in the fog of my mind, I can only see what was once visible:
our simple bed / the coastline / the room with only the sound of a wooden flute

INSTRUCTIONS ON HOW TO LEAVE A TOWN

^

now you have to go back through Ohio just to manage a few sweaters because
it's getting cold out there

pack two grey-green duffels / most of your clothes are torn
what else   do you have to show for yourself
stay in motels   drink bourbon & cut your fingertips on
the zippers of your jeans / throw the oranges at the
ships on the walls   forget her

^

her touch—nearly seven hundred days away / the desk littered with candles &
letters / last night folk music & a light bulb   swinging   humming

sink backed up & the water flooded the dirty blue tiles—you just ducked out

in another town you can imagine fresh basil in the kitchen window   orange peels
ground down to dust   bicycles   farmland   the peripheral at peace with
the eventual

^

you could show up at someone's door   unannounced by the wind

∧

collect weeds as though they are scarce

sleep next to the man who takes care of the trees   the edge is close

between two bodies   smokestacks line the sky

∧

troubled by your body, you're trembling at the gas station

stay in a poorly insulated farmhouse north of the city

wake to a lack of rain, an unbroken sky

remember the moon from last night
that seemed to drift

if god were uneasy
you would not know

THE DISTANCE

I don't want anyone to know anything about me anymore—
& that does include the sound of crescent grass sweeping past my body
            or the eleventh day not having stepped foot outside the room
you ride a bus across rural Pennsylvania
                    it is the distance

                                    that keeps us awake

we are briefly

here

I have not walked into water

wearing my clothes

for a while now

the fire pit

is filled with snow / a glimpse

of the receding house

a piling up of letters / if it were possible to

speak for your absence / there

would be no use for windows

no use

for brass bells or train trestles /

bread

is one elucidation

as well as dust, or the history thereof

I still walk into the house

that my father warns is made

of urchin spines

INTERIORS

in a drawing your face is

tired /   chest

flat

that night when

you pressed my body into the screen door

hard enough

for the rust to measure on my skin

in the kitchen the okra

burned

you took off your

bind / shirt

knotted my hair as you wound it around your small fist

AWAY

frost on the rearview mirror
solitude: blue & rational
in a stranger's window

who says we are apart
there are so many ways to remember
the days covered in sapphire dust

to stay in bed with rye bread & marijuana
in a dream you take me to a lighthouse
[all of my wishes go unattended]

these years   a road of fog
where envelopes rise from the ground
& I fumble with the keys again

III

in this windy nest
open your hungry
mouth in vain . . .
Issa, stepchild bird

—Issa

ENTRY FOR THE BRUTALITY OF THE LETTER ON THE WASHBASIN

hands poised like a rabbit's mouth—again, tinsel, piss, desire ground up in salt—
when I get turned on I put on records—when someone is left sometimes a letter—
the dreariness of a letter, all the words stacked up like a chimney—you exhale
somewhere in a field, everything out of you—how you begin to see someone who
can't stop saying she's in danger—it's not difficult to love

WHAT CAME BETWEEN US

∧

it is not possible in this market
to make the leaves caught in vortices
into something anyone can possibly

own

∧

at first we both
misunderstood when she
took the twin map books
& swallowed them completely

∧

you recite Lorca while they cut away the trees

∧

finally—it doesn't hurt when you speak

clouds open to fjords of wise blue

∧

I'd rather be the strand of hair caught in the stigma of
a sunflower   I don't want a gender or work that can pass

as work (because greed is real)—you step off the plank into

silver

water

∧

a man in a brown, musty truck yells
fucking faggot out the window
& I fall into concession:

I couldn't make a dent
walking home from the post office box
even if I held onto his hitch until let go

∧

I try to taste the smoke in the snow for the fourth night

∧

sometimes I would mount you
like a stag—

we would lie in bed with
the sound of foghorns

EARTH AT UNREST

you have given me
the pale slice of ginger
for the comparison of tongue

my mother who
uses clay to make
a sturdy wall

mostly though, the body
rounding
along the bend
of the landscape

the earth at unrest,
stones with moss,
taste of a bleeding lip

the land with songs
underneath

the land with azalea
ache of azalea

BIRTHRIGHT

all day I walk on dark roads
        in a dream a family takes me fishing then to spend the night at a cousin's house
          he is tall & has a buzz cut with a small white-blond tail of hair down his
neck
          we drive in a truck without headlights   in the back bed four dogs
    bark
      when I think of my real mother she is often wearing a bandanna
the land around her is mossy   there are a thousand coins falling to her
        it's the dream that lets me forget the housepainter who stole money
from my mother & how she is not well in spirit

the fishing lake is dark, cloudy
        I take off my shirt & slip the bandanna from around my hair
      I am young I wade in

from underwater I hear men's voices mostly—my uncles, maybe my father
I can see thin silver fish with deep gills swimming close to the surface—
                they sift through my fingers

ERASURE(S)

white arrows of
    lichen fault the tree

        you have a lover who keeps half of my name in her name
        that's where I'm buried then

we cannot dissolve the highway between us
        or erase the damselflies tireless at the dog's ears

            we cannot fade the wind that echoes sober through the landscape
            or thaw any pinprick of light into a horizontal beam

                though I will try
                again

ROTARY

clothed & sheltered
days empty of you

I draw the calendar as vessels
put clay slip on my legs so moving is heavy in real time

we saw the Sophie Calle exhibit with the rotary telephone on the bed, repeating—
all of those lonely photographs & you just kissed me hard against the back wall

ECHO

does your hair look ruddy in the twilight / I have deftly let go of some thousand
days inward   there are sharp branches   fleets of red buds & hollow buildings

I no longer know how long the echo takes beneath the bridge to reach the air not beneath
the bridge

we have to make what wants to be made

∧

[long pause to clear the brush]

NOT URGENT

looking downwards

the smell of my own breath

in the snowy field

—Hashimoto Takako

∧

scrub off the wrists

a pallet knife scrapes the dissolving pubic bone

in a place where I make no mistakes we climb

ladders into the unhinging sky & our arteries release honey

not now—

though not now

∧

rain not like hands / tired early

this morning I drink tea nearly red

look up at the trees with occasional amber leaves:

yes, I am still in my body

the second time

∧

after I kiss her

she says that my face is pale

I move the birch logs
w/out question

ask, quietly—
who owns me?

EVEN IN GRIEF

the lithograph of two women blowing smoke
onto each other's skin
each passing
morning
without you

a weaving of reeds covers the house
no letters

/

this flint
of morning light

I WILL BE YOUR MIRROR

∧

you tremble only slightly
in the tent in Kentucky over
the underground system of caves

you tear the knotweed
burn the stilt grass

the pages catch fire in the reverse order that they were written
you hang up the phone quickly when you hear what you can
only assemble as a train

∧

in a rented A-frame, you barricade the door
inside, your smallish body is held between the bodies of two butch men you met
online
mercy without commerce

you suck the rain water out of the vortex of lettuce
this isn't a particularly hard place to be   though scarcity
come winter

∧

there is no faith in the shape of an ax
you slice onions, watch   the clouds migrate east

∧

the man whose hair is dry & parted, neat, symmetrical, with the small glass vial of moss around his neck, messages late one night:

I am an animal, you must know

ALTERNATIVE ECONOMIES

I would sell everything I have
clear cut the doubt

a thousand mirrors, strung together
with floss, for the emergence
of your sweaters, elbows
reinforced with leather

hundreds of amber bottles
dug out from an urban trail
if only our tent pitched along a bluff

seven silver dollars for bathing & to
watch you cross your letters

all the fog in my mirror for the house on stilts where
we were naked, sandy, working it out, sadists

a pyramid of copper coins for the scar on the back of your neck

give me distant bells, a film of dunes, your hand fluttering while you sleep or shaking
while you fuck & I'll turn over my collection of field recordings, the storms & the gulls

bartering in tea leaves to pull the stranger out of you

DEAREST, THE SAINTS

rubbings of half a gravestone—   *star*   *bird*   *professor of metaphysics*   I draw

only leaves   I am not & remain the woman who swam with a thousand

     minnows

the students believe   as we turn to Kenyon   that happiness is brief, discursive

even unwarranted / when rain meets the sea I disappear from grief   the

child   *(whose mother has passed out from drink)*   walks alone through the

dunes—I walk near the water   flecked with sails   distant   quiet

from memory   I can still trace the scar on the back of your neck, still your

persistent sweeping of the porch in early hours

though—no-coming, no-going   waves arrive, are present then lost

the mattress is only a sculpture of the mattress   / the birds, woven

the days leading into winter are heavy with jagged brush   when I say your

name aloud the leaf stems quiver

in the wake   my handwriting leaves cinders

DUNES

we floated asleep, as the house beams were carved
with birds & waves through the night

not knowing how to walk through sand dunes
not knowing the sand blue color of your veins

it is tiring to wake each day to the frost
your out breath melancholy, smooth

in the railcar office I do not take off my shirt / an envelope flutters as you turn away—
the lip of where the ordinary paper seals & where it opens, the same

you show me the underused stairwell, suddenly the slight redness of your skin at the collar
below your throat / even when you look away without looking I lose a part of the way

                                        words yield no less an island

CAST OFF

names are costly, they
tore off one wing of

the church & left
the steeple bell

half in the earth
after the rain

look here, your name on
the fall of my tongue

the absence of your hand
fills with wind &

I try to find a good home—
though homes are only root

gardens
I couldn't know

the life between us
is fragile / I keep guard

while you wander
through the pleasure of

books / the taste of
incense on the sides

of the throat & bowing
to the root

to the bone
to the cast-off line

NOTES

TEMPORARY LANDMARK (17)

Italicized text is from Jane Kenyon's poem "Happiness," which appears in *Otherwise: New and Selected Poems* (Graywolf Press, 2005).

VAGABOND (21)

The film referenced is Agnès Varda's *Sans toit ni loi*, ("Without roof or law"). Otherwise, *Vagabond*.

CLIMATES (32)

This poem is an elegy for Nuri Bilge Ceylan's fourth film, *Iklimer*, ("Climates").

UP TO & INCLUDING HER LIMITS (34)

"up to & including her limits" borrows its title from a performance piece by Carolee Schneemann in which she suspended herself in a tree surgeon's harness on a manila rope and lowered her body to make a drawing. She recalls, "my entire body became the agency of visual traces, vestige of the body's energy in motion." The Kitchen, NYC, New York, 1973.

ENTRY FOR THE BRUTALITY OF THE LETTER ON THE WASHBASIN (55) & ROTARY (61)

The exhibit referred to in these poems was Sophie Calle's 2003 show of photographs and text, *Douleur Exquise*, ("Exquisite Pain").

ACKNOWLEDGMENTS

Grateful acknowledgments to the following journals in which some of these poems (or some iteration) first appeared: *Aufgabe, Cream City Review, DIAGRAM, Ecotone, Faultline, Free Verse, Lake Effect, Meridian, So to Speak: A Feminist Review, Sonora Review, Touchstone,* and *Tupelo Quarterly.*

IN GRATITUDE

Through the process of writing this book, I owe gratitude to those who have supported, challenged, provoked, and encouraged me. Thank you for your care, interest and presence in my life and work.

To the many artists, writers, and readers whose advice was invaluable, including: Robert Andrade, Jumay Chu, Cathy Lee Crane, eric cressley, Lynn Emmanuel, Joshua Geldzahler, Jeffrey Gibson, Andrea Hammer, Christopher Holmes, Gabriela Jiménez, Paul Kameen, Baseera Khan, Oliver Khan, Lena Masur, Ruth Oppenheim, Maria Park, Laurie Parker, Lisa Pepper, Robert Pope, Lynn Powell, Nilima Rabl, Farideh Sakhaeifar, Tomaž Šalamun, Ronni Tartlet, Sandy Tseng, Stacey Waite, Rick Wormwood, and Bernard Yenelouis.

To friends in the San Juan Islands, including Suzanne Berry, Carmen Cicotti, Claudia Elwell, Kenny Ferrugiaro, Karen Fisher, Christine Langley, Teri Linneman, Pamela Pauly, Levi Rodriguez, Kai Sanburn, Liz Scranton, Table Studzienko, Cathy Wilson, Steven Wrubleski, and the late Angie Ponder.

Thank you Hester Angus, Samantha Baker, James Bentz, Candice Esposito, Lauren Jesiolowski, Phil Seibel, Tomoko Sherrod, Stacy Torres, Acca Warren, Erin Weller, and Catherine Zagare for your love and support.

To the Astraea Lesbian Foundation for Justice whose generous grant supported my work and helped me stay afloat while I wrote some of the poems in this book.

Thank you to Carl Phillips for seeing this book and to Red Hen Press for seeing it through.

Joe Weller, Libby Clark, and Michael Weller for their warmth & friendship; Darío Núñez-Ameni for a poetics of space; Nina Svatovic, for clarity of heart; Megan Hunter for vision and alignment; Elliot Nappi, for staying true; Vicki Modica, for her compassion and smarts; Robin Hart, for showing up early on (I am so lucky); Sweller Weller, for their tenacity, generosity, and love.

Deborah Jesiolowski, Bernard Jesiolowski, Nika Stokowski, Bianca Jesiolowski, Sierrah Jesiolowski, and Azaeda Raynn, you are my life and my strength.

"earth at unrest" is in loving memory of Lotte Jungmeir McMarlin.

This book is for Rohen (the greyhound), whose wise calm is with me always. Hearts.

BIOGRAPHICAL NOTE

Gabriel Jesiolowski is a queer and feminist artist, writer, designer, and curator. They work in a research-based practice using installation, painting, photography, printed matter, and text to scuffle within the spaces of language and art. Their work has been shown in galleries such as the Dumbo Arts Center, Future Tenants Gallery, and the Flux Factory and appeared in print in *Crossings: A Counter Disciplinary Journal, So to Speak: a Feminist Review,* and *Topos: The International Review of Landscape and Architecture and Urban Design* among others. They were a recent writer-in-residence at The Alice Gallery in Seattle and a 2016 MacDowell fellow. They are poetry editor for Territory. They live and work in Los Angeles and the San Juan Islands.

More of their work can be found at gabrieljesiolowski.com.